Penguins

ALICE TWINE

PowerKiDS press™

New York

For Mrs. von Zumbusch and the Princeton Junior School's "penguin class"

Published in 2008 by The Rosen Publishing Group, Inc.
29 East 21st Street, New York, NY 10010

First Edition

Editor: Amelie von Zumbusch
Book Design: Julio Gil
Photo Researcher: Nicole Pristash

Photo Credits: Cover, pp. 1, 11 © Thorsten Milse/Getty Images; p. 5 © www.istockphoto.com/Melody Kerchhoff; pp. 7, 9, 15 Shutterstock.com; p. 13 © www.istockphoto.com/Alexander Kautz; p. 17 © www.istockphoto.com/Roman Kazmin; p. 19 © www.istockphoto.com/Wolfgang Schoenfeld; p. 21 © Morales/Age Fotostock; p. 23 © Getty Images.

Library of Congress Cataloging-in-Publication Data

Twine, Alice.
  Penguins / Alice Twine. — 1st ed.
     p. cm. — (Baby animals)
  Includes index.
  ISBN 978-1-4042-4147-3 (library binding)
  1. Penguins—Infancy—Juvenile literature. I. Title.
  QL696.S473T95 2008
  598.47'139—dc22

                                                2007021209

Manufactured in the United States of America

Contents

Baby penguins are called chicks. Penguin chicks are covered in soft, fluffy **down**.

4

There are many kinds of penguins. King penguin chicks have brown down.

Chinstrap penguins build piles of small rocks to make nests for their chicks.

Emperor penguins, like this chick, live in snowy Antarctica. They are the biggest kind of penguin.

Not all penguins live in cold Antarctica. These African penguin chicks live in warm southern Africa.

Penguins lay eggs. They sit on the eggs to keep them warm. In time, chicks break out of the eggs.

15

Penguin mothers and fathers make sure their chicks stay warm. They also **groom**, or clean, the chicks.

17

Penguins eat fish and other sea animals. Adult penguins feed their chicks from their own stomach.

Some kinds of penguin chicks form groups called **crèches**.

In time, penguin chicks grow smooth **feathers** in place of down. Then, the penguins learn to swim.

Words to Know

crèche

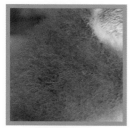

down

feathers

groom

Index

Web Sites

Due to the changing nature of Internet links, PowerKids Press has developed an online list of Web sites related to the subject of this book. This site is updated regularly. Please use this link to access the list:
www.powerkidslinks.com/baby/peng/

24